Anonymous

The History of Bacon's and Ingram's Rebellion in Virginia

In 1675 and 1676

Anonymous

The History of Bacon's and Ingram's Rebellion in Virginia
In 1675 and 1676

ISBN/EAN: 9783337209605

Printed in Europe, USA, Canada, Australia, Japan

Cover: Foto ©ninafisch / pixelio.de

More available books at **www.hansebooks.com**

THE HISTORY

OF

BACON'S AND INGRAM'S REBELLION

IN VIRGINIA,

In 1675 and 1676.

CAMBRIDGE:

PRESS OF JOHN WILSON AND SON.

1867.

From the "Proceedings of the Massachusetts Historical Society"

For 1866–1867.

PREFATORY NOTE.

THE somewhat famous episode in the history of Virginia, known as "Bacon's Rebellion," took place in the years 1675 and 1676. In the latter part of the year 1676, Bacon died; and, by January following, his lieutenant-general, Ingram (whose true name, says Beverly, was Johnson), and his major-general, Walklett, had surrendered, and peace was restored.

For the character of the leader, Colonel Nathaniel Bacon, — who is said to have "been brought up at one of the Inns of Court in England," and to have been "young, bold, active, of an inviting aspect and powerful elocution," — and for the causes which brought about this popular rising against Sir William Berkeley, we would refer to the "History of Virginia," by Robert Beverly (an almost contemporary writer), and also to the later Histories of that State, by John Burk and by Charles Campbell. See also, in the first volume of Force's "Historical Tracts," a narrative, entitled "The Beginning, Progress, and Conclusion of Bacon's Rebellion," and said to have been written thirty years after the events took place; also, in the same volume, a

paper called, "An Account of Our Late Troubles in
Virginia, written in 1676, By Mrs Ann Cotton, of Q.
Creeke."

The manuscript, from which the following narrative
is printed, is evidently contemporaneous with the events
described, or written not long after their occurrence.
It is in the form of a small octavo, the text, with the
heading, measuring five inches and a half by three and
a half, not paged. Portions of it are wanting. Fifty-
two pages survive. The chirography is remarkably dis-
tinct. Several leaves being destroyed at the beginning
and the end, there is no title, except the running-title
on each page, viz., "The Indians Proseedings," "Ingram's Proceedings," &c., as in the reprint. Upon the
outside of the brown paper cover, in a later hand, is
written "Bacons proccedi[ngs,] July 27, 1764." Many
of the remaining leaves are much injured by time.

The unknown writer of the manuscript, near the
close, on page 49 of this volume, says that Major
Page, one of the rebels executed, was "once my sarvant at his first coming into the countrey." In "A List
of those that have been executed for ye late Rebellion
in Virginia," furnished by Governor Berkeley, and pub-
lished in the first volume of Force's "Historical Tracts,"
is the following: "One Page, a carpenter, formerly my
servant," &c. The query is at once suggested, whether
Sir William Berkeley, the Governor, was the author of
this manuscript. It was evidently written by one who
did not sympathize with the rebel movement, but from
some criticisms, in the narrative, on the motives and
conduct of Sir William, it seems hardly possible that

he could have been the writer. Sir William died, says Campbell, on the 13th of July, 1677.

This narrative was first printed in the First Volume of the Second Series of the Massachusetts Historical Society's Collections, in 1814, from the manuscript just described, which was communicated to the Society by the late Hon. Josiah Quincy, then a member of Congress from the State of Massachusetts. Mr. Quincy received the manuscript from the Hon. William A. Burwell, member of Congress from the State of Virginia, accompanied by the following letter: —

WASHINGTON, December 20th, 1812.

DEAR SIR, — The manuscript copy of "Bacon and Ingram's Rebellion" was found among the papers of the late Captain Nathaniel Burwell, of King-William County. I have not been able to obtain many particulars from his family relative to it.

At the close of the war, he heard of its existence in an old and respectable family of the Northern Neck of Virginia, and procured it for his amusement: he entertained no doubt of its antiquity, and valued it on that account.

From the appearance of the work, the minute and circumstantial detail of facts, the orthography, and the style, I am perfectly satisfied his opinion was correct. I hope it will be found worthy of a place in the valuable Collections of the Society to which you belong.

Permit me to offer my best wishes for the success of your labors.

Yours respectfully,

WILLIAM A. BURWELL, of Virginia.

The attention of the Massachusetts Historical Society having been recently called to this manuscript, with a view of restoring it to the family of Mr. Burwell, or of depositing it in the Library of the Virginia Historical Society, where it has since been placed, a careful collation of it with the printed copy was made by the

Assistant Librarian, Dr. John Appleton, and a great many errors and some omissions in the latter were discovered. The required corrections were made in a copy of the printed volume; and, in view of their number and importance, the Committee, to whom the subject was referred, decided to have the paper reprinted before the manuscript should be returned to Virginia. It has accordingly been printed in a volume of the Society's Proceedings, under the date of August, 1867; and two hundred copies have been struck off in a separate form.

For the Committee of Publication,

CHARLES DEANE.

Boston, September 20, 1867.

[THE HISTORY OF BACON'S AND INGRAM'S REBELLION.]

[" *The Indians Proseedings.*"]

. . . .*

for there owne security. They found that there store was too short to indure a long Seige, with out makeing emty belles and that emty belies, makes weake hearts, which all ways makes an unfit Serving Man to wāte upon the God of war. Therefore they were resalue, before that there spirits were downe, to doe what they could to keepe there stores up; as oppertunity should befriend them. And all though they were by the Law of Arms (as the case now stood) prohibited the hunting of wilde Deare, they resalued to see what good might be don by hunting tame Horsses. Which trade became their sport soe loñ, that those who came on Horsback to the seige, began to feare the should be compeld to trot hom a foot, and glad if they seap'd so too: for these belegured A neglected seige. blades made so many salleys, and the beseigers kep such neglegent gards, that there was very few days past without som remarkeable mischeife. But what can hould out all ways? euen stone walls yeilds to the not to be gaine-saide summons of time. And all though it is saide that the Indians doth the least minde their Bellies (as being content with a litle) of any people in the world, yet now there bellies began to minde them, and there stomacks too, which began to be more inclineable to peace, then war; which was the cause (no more Horss flesh being to be had) that they sent out 6 of their Worawances (cheife The Indians send out . . there cheif men to . . men) to commence a treaty. What the Artickles were, that they brought aloñ with them, to treate of, I do not know; but certainly . . . . they were so unacceptable to the English, that they caused the Commissioners braines to be knock'd out, for dictateing so badly to there tongues; which yet, 'tis posible, exprest more reason then the English had, to prove the lawfullness of this action, being Diametrecall to the Law of Arms.

* Where dots are inserted, the manuscript is either torn or illegible; where brackets are used, the words are supplied by the Editors; where the original is indistinct, italics are employed. — Eds.

This strange action put those in the Fort to there trumps, haueing thus lost som of their prime court cards, without a faire dealeing. They could not well tell what interpretation *to put upon it* (nor indeed, nobody ell-) and very faine they wo[uld] . . . why those, whom they sent out with a [view] *to suplicate* a peace should be worss delt with then [those who] were sent out with a sword to denounce a war ; but, [no one] could be got to make inquirye into the reason of this . . . which put them upon a ressalution to forsake there [station, and] not to expostulate the cause any further. Haueing [made] this resalution, and destroyed all things in the fort, that might be servisable to the English, they bouldly, undiscovered, slip through the Leagure (leave-ing the English to prossecute the seige, as Schogin's wife brooded the eggs that the Fox had suck'd) in the passing of which they knock'd ten men o'th head, who lay carelessly asleep in there way.

The Indians forsake [the] Fort.

Now all though it might be saide that the Indians went there ways emty handed, in regard they had left all there plunder and welth behinde them in the fort, yet it cannot be thought that they went away emty hearted : For though that was pritty well drained from it's former curage, through those inconvenencies that they had bin subjected to, by the seige, yet in ye roome thereof, rather then the venticles should lie voide, they had stowed up so much mallize, entermixt with a ressalu-tion of revenge, for the affrunt that the English had put upon them, in killing there messingers of peace, that they resalued to commence a most barberous and most bloody war.

The Indians resolue to re-venge them-selues on the English.

The Beseigers haueing spent a grate deale of ill imployed time in pecking at the huske, and now findeing the shell open, and mising the expected prey, did not a litle woonder what was be com of the lately impounded Indinans, who, though at present the could not be seene, yet it was not long before that they were heard off, and felt too. For in a very short time they had, in a most inhumane maner, murthered no less then 60 innocent people, no ways guilty of any actuall injury don to these ill disarning, brutish heathen. By the blood of these poore soules, they thought that the wandering ghosts of those there Commissioners, before mentioned, might be atton'd, and lade downe to take there repose in the dismall shades of death, and they, at present, not obliged for to prossecute any further revenge. Therefore to prove whether the English was as redy for a peace, as themselues, they send in there remonstronce in the name of there [Chief, (ta]ken by an Eng-lish interpreter,) unto the Governour [of Verg]inia, with whom he expostulates in this sort. Wh[at was it] that moved him to take up

The Indians . . . to justi-fy there Pro-seedings.

Arms, against him, his pr[ofessed] friend, in the behalfe of the Marylanders, his profes[sed] ene]mies, contrary to that league made betwene
[him] and himselfe? Declares as well his owne as su[bjects] greife
to finde the Verginians, of Frinds, without any cause giuen, to becom
his foes, and to be so eager in their groundless quarill, as to persew
the chase into anothers dominions: Complaines, that his mesingers of
peace, were not oneley murthered by the English, but the fact coun-
tinanced by the Governour's Connivance: For which, seeing no other
ways to be satisfied, he had revenged him self, by killing 10 for one of
the Verginians, such being the disperportion betwene his grate men
murther'd, and those, by his command, slane. That now, this being
don, if that his honour would alow him a valluable satisfaction for the
damage he had sustained by the war, and no more concerne himselfe
in the Marylanders quarill, he was content to renew and confirm the
ancient league of amety; other ways him selfe, and those whom he had
ingaged to his intress (and there owne) were resalued to fite it out to
the Last man.

These proposealls not being assented to by the English, as being
derogetory and point blanke, both to honour and intress, these Indians
draw in others (formerly in subjection to the Verginians) to there The Re...
trance...
by the...
aides: which being conjoyned (in seperate and united parties) they
dayly commited abundance of ungarded and un revenged murthers,
upon the English; which they perpretated in a most barberous and
horid maner. By which meanes abundance of the Fronteare Plantations became eather depopulated by the Indians cruletys [sic], or
desarted by the Planters feares, who were compelled to forsake there
abodes, to finde security for there lives; which they were not to part
with, in the hands of ye Indiands, but under the worst of torments.
For these brutish and inhumane brutes, least their cruilties might not
be thought cruill enough, they devised a hundred ways to torter and The Cruel-
ties of ye In-
dians.
torment those poore soules with, whose reched fate it was to fall in to
there unmercyfull hands. For som, before that they would deprive
them of there lives, they would take a grate deale of time to deprive them first of there skins, and if that life had not, throug[h the
ang]uish of there paine, forsaken there tormented bodyes, they [with]
there teeth (or som instrument,) teare the nailes of [their fingers and
their] toes, which put the poore sufferer to a wo[ful condition. One
was prepared for the fla]mes at Iames Towne, who indured [much,
but found means] to escape. Those who had the . . . . . . another world,
was to haue . . . . . . to be attributed to . . . . . . there more then can

...... xpire with ... or other wayes to be slane out rite, for least that there Deaths should be attributed unto som more mercyfull hands then theares, for to put all out of question, they would leaue som of there brutish Markes upon there fenceless bodies, that might testifye it could be none but they who had commited the fact.

And now it was that the poore distresed and dubly afflicted Planters began to curss and execrate that ill manidged buisness at the Fort. There eryes were reitterated againe and againe, both to God and man for releife. But no appearcance of long wish'd for safety ariseing in the Horrison of there hopes, they were redy, could they haue tould which way, to leaue all and forsake the Collony; rather then to stay and be expos'd to the crewiltys of the barberous heathen.

At last it was concluded, as a good expedient for to put the coun-
Forts to be [buil]t.
trey in to som degree of safety, for to plant Forts upon the Fronteres, thinkeing there by to put a stop unto the Indians excurssions: which after the expence of a grate deale of time and charge, being finished, came short of the designed ends. For the Indians quickly found out where about these Mouse traps were sett, and for what purpose, and so resalued to keepe out of there danger; which they might easely ennough do, with out any detriment to there designes. For though here by they were compeld (tis posible) to goe a litle about, yet they never thought much of there labour, so long as they were not debar'd from doing of Mischeife; which was not in the power of these forts to prevent: .For if that the English did, at any time, know that there
Not vallued by the Indians.
was more ways in to the wood then one, to kill Deare, the Indians found more then a thousand out of the wood, to kill Men, and not com neare the danger of the forts neather.

The small good that was by most expected, and now by [them expe]rienc'd from these useless fabricks (or castells, if a . . . a marvellous discontent amongst the people. . . . the charge would be grate, and the benifitt . . . arise out of these wolfe-pi . . . . . . came every day losers; and . . . . . . Banke, if it do not ine . . . . . . to cast about for so . . . . . . lost. It vext t[he hearts of many tha they should] be compeld to worke all the day, (nay all the yeare), for to reward those Mole-catchers at the forts, (no body knew for what,) and at night could not finde a place of safety to lie downe in, to rest there wery bones, for feare they should be shatter'd all to peices by the Indians; upon which consideration the thought it best to petition the downe fall of these useless (and like to be) chargeable fabricks, from whose continuance they could neather expect prollitt nor safety.

But for the effecting of this buisness, they found them selues un-   The Forts
disliked by
the English.
der a very grate disadvantage. For though it may be more easier to
cast downe, then irect, well cemented structurs, yet the rule doth not
hould in all cases. For it is to be understood that these Forts were
contrived, eather by the sole command of the Governour, or other
ways by the advice of those whose judgments, in this affaire, he approved off; eather of which was now, they being don, his owne emediate act, as they were don in his name; which to haue undon, at the
simple request of the people, had bin, in efect, to haue undon that
Repute he all ways held, in the peoples judgment, for a wise Man; and
better that they should suffer som small inconvenencies, then that he
should be counted less diserning then those, who, till now, were
counted more then halfe blinde. Besides, how should he satisfie his
honour with the undertakers of the worke? If the peoples petition
should be granted, they must be disapointed, which would haue bin
litle less then an undoeing to the allsoe. in there expectation of proffitt
to be raised from the worke. Here by the people quickly found them
selues in an errour, when that they apprehended what a strong founda-
tion the Forts were irected upon, honour and proffitt, against which all
there saping and mincing had no power to over turne; they haueing no
other ingredience to makeing up there fire works with but prayers,
and miss spent teares and intreties; which haueing vented to no purpose, and finding there condition every whit as bad, if not worse since,
as before, the forts were made, they resalued . . . le patience was set to
worke.

. . . . . . many to hope in the countin- . . . . . of no long being in the Bacon ap-
[pe]ares
against the
Indians.
cou- . . . . . . state: and nerely related to one . . . . . . guity. A Man he
was of larger . . . . . . hich rendred him indeared (if not . . . . . . not for
any thing he had yet don, as the cause of there affections, but what they
expected he would doe to disarve there devotion; while with no common
zeale, they send up there reitterated prayers, first to him self, and next
to Heaven, that he may becom there Gardian Angle, to protect them
from the cruilties of the Indians, against whom this Gentiman had a
perfict antipothey.

It seemes, in the first rise of the War, this Gentiman had made
som overtures, unto the Governour, for a Commission, to go and put a
stop to the Indians proseedings. But the Governour, at present, eather
not willing to commence the quarill (on his part) till more suteable
reasons prisented, for to urge his more severe prosecution of the same,
against the heathen: or that he douted Bacons temper, as he appear'd

Populerly inclin'd: A constetution not consistant with the times, and the peoples di-possitions; being generally discontented, for want of timely provissions against the Indians, or for Aūnall impositions lade upon them, too grate (as they saide) for them to beare, and against which they had som considerable time complained, without the least redress. For these, or som other reasons, the Governour refused to comply with Bacon's proposalls. Which he lookeing upon as an undervalluing as well to his parts, as a disperidgment to his pretentions, hee in som elated and passionate expressions, sware Commission or no Commission, the next man or woman that he heard of that should be kild by the Indians, he would goe out against them, though but 20 men would adventure the servis with him. Now it so unhappylie fell out, that the next person that the Indians did kill, was one of his owne ffamiley. Where upon haueing got together som 70 or 80 persons, most good Howsekeepers, well armed, and seeing that he could not legally procure a Commission (after som struglings with the Governour (. . . Scuffell) and som of his best friends, co . . . terprise, he applyes hi . . . . . . his oath, and so forth . . . . . . ans.

The Governour could not . . . . . . this insolent deportment of Bac . . . . . . ed at his proscedings. Which . . . . . . insteade of seekeing meanes to appease his anger, they devised meanes to increase it, by frameing specious pretences, which they grounded upon the bouldness of Bacons actions, and the peoples affections. They began (som of them) to haue Bacons Merits in mistrust, as a Luminary that thretned an eclips to there risceing gloryes. ·For though he was but a yong man, yet they found that he was master and owner of those induments which constitutes a Compleate Man, (as to intrinceecalls) wisdom to apprehend and descretion to chuse. By which imbelishments (if he should continue in the Governours favour) of Seniours they might becom juniours, while there yoūger Brother, through the nimbleness of his wit, might steale away that blessing, which they accounted there owne by birth-right. This rash proscedings of Bacon, if it did not undo himselfe, by his faileing in the enterprise, might chance to undo them in the affections of the people; which to prevent, they thought it conduceable to there intress and establishment, for to get yᵉ Governour in the minde to proclame him a Rebell; as knowing that once being don, since it could not be don but by and in the Governours name, it must needs breed bad blodd betwene Bacon and Sʳ William, not easely to be purged. For though Sʳ William might forgiue, what Bacon, as yet, had acted; yet it might be questionable whether Bacon might forget

what Sir William had don: However, according to there desires, Forces...
Bacon and all his adhereance was proclamed a Rebell, May the 29, to reduce
and forces raised to reduce him to his duty. With which the Gov- Bacon.
ernour advanced from the Midle Plantation* to finde him out, and if
neede was to fight him, if the Indians had not knock'd him, and those
with him, on the head, as som were in hope they had don, and which
by som was ernistly desired.

After som few days the Governour retracts his march, (a jurnye of
som 30 or 40 miles) to meet with the Assembley, now redy to sit
downe at our Metropollis, while Bacon in the meane time meets with Bacon
the Indians, upon whom he falls with abundance of ressalution and me[ets] with
gallentrey (as his owne party relates it) in there fastness: killing a the Indians.
grate many, and blowing up there Magazene of Arms and Pouder,
to a considerable quantity ... y his self, no less then 4000 weight.
This [being done, and all his] Provissions spent, he returns hom to his
... e, where he submits him selfe to be chosen Bur[gess of t]he County
in which he did live, contrary to his qualifications, take him as he was
formerly one of the Councell of State, or as hee was now a proclamed
Rebell. How ever, he applyes him selfe to the performance of that
trust reposed in him, by the people, if he might be admited into the
Howse. But this not faging according to his desire, though according
to his expectation, and he remaneing in his sloope, (then at Ancor Bacon taken
before the Towne) in which was about 30 Gentmen besides himselfe, prisoner.
he was there surprised with the rest, and made prissoner, som being
put into Irons: in which condition they remaned som time, till all
things were fitted for the triall. Which being brought to a day of Brought
heareing, before the Governour and Councell, Bacon was not onely upon his
aequited and pardoned all misdemeniors, but restored to the Councell triall and
Table as before; and not onely, but promised to haue a Commission aequited.
signed the Monday following (this was on the Saterday) as Generall June 10.
for the Indian war, to the universall satisfaction of the people, who promised a
passionately desired the same; witnessed by the ginerall acclameations Commission.
of all then in towne.

And here who can do less then wonder at the muteable and imper-
menent deportments of that blinde Godes Fortune; who, in the morning loades Man with disgraces, and ere night crownes him with
honours: Somtimes depressing, and againe ellivateing, as her fickle
humer is to smile or frowne, of which this Gen'smans fate was a kinde

---

* Williamsburg. See Beverly's History of Virginia. — EDS.

3

of an Epittemey, in the severall vicissetudes and changes he was subjected to in a very few dayes. For in the morning, before his triall, he was, in his Enimies hopes, and his Friends feares, judged for to recene the Gurdian due to a Rebell (and such hee was proclamed to be) and ere night, crowned the Darling of the Peoples hopes and desires, as the onely man fitt in Verginia, to put a stop unto the bloody ressalutions of the Heathen : And yet againe, as a fuller manifestation of Fortune's inconstancye, with in two or three days, the peoples hopes, and his desires, were both frusterated by the Governours refuseing to signe the promised Commission. At which being disgusted, though at present he desembled ... so well as he could, (and tis supposed that w ... he beggs leaue of the Governour for to be despence ... his servis at the Councell table, to vissit his L ... he saide, had informed him, was indisposed, as to her ... which request the Governour (after som contest with his owne thoughts) granted, contrary to the advise of som about him, who suspected Bacons designes, and that it was not so much his Lady's sickness, as the distempers of a troubled minde, that caused him to with draw to his owne house, and that this was the truth, with in a few days was manifested, when that he returned to Towne at the head of 500 Men in Arms.

The Governo[ur] refuseth to signe the Commission.

Bacon disgusted.

The Governour did not want intillegence of Bacons designes, & therefore sent out his summons for Yorke Traine Bands to reinforce his gards, then at Towne. But the time was so short, (not above 12 howers warning) and those that appeared at the Randevouze made such a slender number, that under 4 Insignes there was not mustered above 100 Soulders, and not one halfe of them sure neather, and all so slugish in there march, that before they could reach towne, by a grate deale, Bacon had enter'd the same, and by force obtained a Commition, calculated to the hight of his owne desires. With which Commission, (such as it was,) being invested, hee makes redy his provissions, fills up his Companies to the designed number (500 in all) and so applies him selfe to those serrises the Countrey expected from him. And, first, for ye secureing the same from the excursions of the Indians, in his absence (and such might be expected) he commissionated severall persons, (such as he could confide in) in every respectiue county, with select companies of well armed men, to range the Forists, swomps, thickits, and all such suspected places where the Indiands might haue any shelter for the doeing of mischeife. Which proseedings of his put so much curage into the Planters, that they began to applye them selues to there accustomed imployments in there plantations : which

Bacon returnes to Towne at the head of 500 men, and forceath a Commission.

till now they durst not do, for feare of being knock'd on the head, as,
God knowes. too many were, before these orders were observed.

While the Generall (for so was Bacon now denominated by vertue
of his Commission) was sedulous in these affaires, & fitting his provissions, about the head of Yorke River, in order to his advance against
the Indians; the Governour was stearcing quite contrary courses. He
was once more perswaded (but for what reasons not visible) to pro-
claime Bacon a Rebell againe. And now since his absence afforded
an advantage, to raise the countrey upon him, so soone as he should
returne tired and exhausted by his toyle and labour in the Indian war.
For the puting this councell in execution, the Governour steps ouer into
Gloster County, (a place the best replenished for men, arms, and affections of any County in Verginia,) all which the Governour summons   The Govern-
to giue him a meeteing at a place & day assigned, where being met,   our sum-
according to the summons, the Governours proposalls was so much   mons in the
                                                                        Gloster men
disrellished, by the wholl convention, that they all disbanded to   to the Court
there owne aboades, after there promise past to stand by, and assist   house.
the Governoure, against all those who should go about to rong, eather
his parson, or debase his Authority; unto which promise they an-
next, or subioyned severall reasons why they thought it not, at present, convenient to declare them selues against Bacon, as he was now
advanceing against the common enimy, who had in a most barberous maner murthered som hundreds of o[r] deare Breatheren and Countrey Men. and would, if not prevented by God. and the endeviours of
good men, do there utmost for to cut of the wholl Collony. There-   The Glosters
fore they did thinke that it would be a thing inconsistant with reason, men's pro-
                                                                         testation.
if that they, in this desperate coniunture of time, should go and ingage
themselves one against another; from the result of which proseedings,
nothing could be expected but ruing and destruction unto both, to the
one and the other party, since that it might reasonably be conceued,
that while they should be exposeing there brests against one anothers
wepons, the barberous and common enimy (who would make his disadvantages [sic] by our disadvantages) should be upon there backs to
knock out there brains. But if it should so hapen (as they did hope
it would never so hapen) that the Generall after the Indian war was
finished. should attempt any thing against his Hon[r] person or Gover-
ment. that then they would rise up in arms, with a joynt consent, for
the prisarvation of both.

Since the Governour could obtaine no more, he was, at present, to
rest himselfe contented with this, while those who had advised him to

these undertakeings, was not a litle dissatisfide to finde the event not
to answer there expectations. But he at present, seeing there was no
more to be don, since he wanted a power to haue that don, which was
esteemed the maine of the affaires, now in hand to be don, namely,
the gaineing of the Gloster men, to do what he would haue don, he
thought it not amiss to do what he had a power to do, and that was

Bacon pro-
[cla]imed a
Tratour.

once more to proclame Bacon a Tratour, which was performed in all
publick places of meetings in these parts. The noyse of which proc-
lameation, after that it had past the admireation of all that were not
aquainted with the reasons that moued his honr to do what he had now
don, soone reached the Generall cares, not yet stopt up from lisning
to apparent dangers.

This strange and unexpected news put him, and som with him,
shrodely to there trumps, beleveing that a few such deales, or shuffles
(call them which you please) might quickly ring the cards, and game
too, out of his hand. He perceued that he was falne (like the corne
betwene the stones) so that if he did not looke the better about him,
he might chance to be ground to powder. He knew that to haue a
certaine enimy in his frunt, and more then uncertaine friends in his
reare, portended no grate security from a violent death, and that there
could be no grate differance betwene his being wounded to death in his
brest, with bows and Arows, or in the back with Guns and Musquit
bullits. He did see that there was an abseluted necessity of destroy-
ing the Indians, for the prisarvation of the English, and that there was
som care to be taken for his owne and soulders safety, otherways that
worke must be ill don, where the laberours are mad criples, and compeld, insteade of a sword, to betake them selues to a c[ru]tch. It
vext him to the hert (as he was heard to say) f[or] to thinke, that while
he was a hunting Wolves, Tygers and Foxis, which dayly destroyed
our ha[r]mless Sheep and Lamb[s,] that hee, and those with him,
should be persued in the re[are], with a full crye, as a more salvage
or no less rave[nous] beast. But to put all out of doubt, and himselfe
into . . . gree of safety, since he could not tell but that som [whom]
he had left behinde, might not more desire his de[ath,] then to here
that by him the Indians were dest[royed, he] forth with (after a short
consultation held with [som of his soulde]rs) countermarcheth his
Army, and in a triee . . . with them at the midle Plantation,* a place
sit[uated in the] very heart of the Countrey.

---

* Williamsburg. — EDS.

The first thing that Bacon fell upon (after [that he had] setled himselfe at the Midle Plantation) was [to prepare] his Remonstrance, and that as well against [the Governo]urs Paper of the 29 of May, as in answer to th[e Governours pro]clamation. Puting both papers upon these D[eclarations, he asks] Whether Parsons wholly devoted to there Kin[g and coun]trey, haters of all sinester, and by respects, am[ing on]ly at the Conntreys good, and indeviouring to th[e utmost of there] power, to the haserd of there lives & fortunes, ... destroy those that are in Arms against King & . . . that never plotted, contrived, nor indevioured . . . ion, detrement or rong of any of his Majesties [subjects, in] there lives, names, fortunes, or estates, can desarue the appellations of Rebells and Traters? He cites the wholl country to testifye his & his soulders peaceable behaviours ; upbrades som in Authorety with the meaness of there parts ; others, now welthey, with the meaness of there estates, when the came first in to the Country ; and questions by what just ways, or meanes, they haue obtained the same; and whether they haue not bin the spunges that haue suck'd up & devoured the common tresūrye ? Questions what Arts, Ciences, Schooles of learning or Ma[n]ufactures hath bin promoted by any now in Authorety? Iustifyes his aversion (in generall) against the Indians ; Upbrades the Governour for manetaineing there quarill (though never so unjust) against the Christians rites and intress ; His refuseing to admit an English man's oath against an Indian, when that an [In]dians word shall be a sufficient proofe against an [En]glish Man : Saith som thing against the Governour [con]cerning the Beaver trade, as not in his power to de . . . off, as being a Monopley appertaineing to the Cro[wn] : Questions whether the Traders at the heads of the . . . s do not buy & sell the blood of there deare Brther , . . untrey men : Araignes one Coll: Coles ascertion [for sayi]ng that the English are bound to protect the Ind[ians] . . . or to the haserd of there blood ; and so conclu[des] [with a]n appeale to King and Parliament, where he [has no doubt] but that his and the Peoples cause will be im[partially h]eard.

[Bacon's declaration.]

[After this manner] the Game beginns, in which (though never so . . . the one side must be, undoubtedly, losers. This . . . nce of Bacons was but the Præludum (or rath . . . e) to the following Chapter : without which the . . . t (in peoples mindes) be subject to rong interpre . . . other ways look'd upon to be, at best, but Hetro . . . he inditers good meaneing.

. . . his next worke was to invite all that had [any regar]d to them-

selues, or love to there Countrey, the . . . Children, or any other relations; to giue [him a meeting] in his Quarters, at a day named,
then and the[re to consu]lt how to put the countrey in to som degree
of safety, and to indevoure for to stop those imminent dangers, now
thretning the destruction of the wholl Collony, through the bloody
proseedings of the Indians; and (as he said) by Sr William B. doteing
and ireguler actings. Desireing of them not to sit still, in this common time of callamitye, with there hands in there bosums; or as uncon-
cer'd spectaters, stand gazeing upon their approcheing ruinys, and not
lend a hand to squench those flames now likely to consume them and
theres to ashes.

According to the summons, most of the prime Gen'men in these
parts, (where of som were of the Councell of State) gaue Bacon a
meeteing in his quarters, at ye assigned time. Where being met (after
a long Harange by him made, much of the nature of, and to explane
the summons) he desired them to take the same so far in to there consideration, that there might, by there wisdom, som expedient [be]
found out, as well for the countryes securytie against Sr Williams
Ireguler proseedings, as that hee, and Armye, might unmollest prossecute the Indian war. Adiug, that neather him selfe, nor those
under his command, thought it a thing consisting with reason, or common sence, to advance against the common Enimy, and in the meane
time want insureance (when they had don the worke abrode) not to
haue their throtes cut, when they should return hom, by those whoe
had set them to worke: being confident that Sr William and som
others with him, through a sence of their unworantable actions, would
do what was posible to be don, not onely to destroy himself, but others
(privie to their knavereys) now ingaged in the Indian servis with
him.

After that Bacon had urg'd, what he thought meet for ye better cary-
ing on of those affaires, now hammering in his head, it was concluded
by the wholl Convention, that for ye establishing the Generall, and
Army, in a cousistancy of safety, and that as well upon his march
against the Indians, as when that he should returne from the servis,
and allso for the keepeing the Countrey in peace, in his absence, that
there should be a test. or recognition, drawne, and subscribed by the
wholl Countrey, which should oblige then [sic] and every of them, not
to be aideing nor assisting to Sr Will. Berkley (for now he would not
afford him the title of Governour) in any sorte, to the molestation,
hinderance or detriment of the Ginerall and Army. This being as-

sented to, the Clarke of the Assembley was ordred to put the same The Oath projected.
in to forme; which while he was a doeing, the Generall would needs
haue another branch added to the former, viz. That the people should
not onely be obliged not to be aideing unto S^r W: B. against the Generall, but that by the force of this Recognition, they should be obliged
to rise in Arms against him, if he with armed forces should offer to
resist the Generall, or desturb the Countries peace, in his absence: and
not onely so, but (to make the ingagement Al-a-mode [*sic*] Rebellion)
he would haue it added, that if any f' ·ces should be sent out of England, at ye request of Sr William, or other ways to his aide, that they
were likewise to be aposed, till such time as the Countrys cause should
be sent hom, and reported to his most Sacred Majesty.

These two last branches of this Bugbeare did marvellously startle
the people, especially the very last of all, yet for to giue the Generall
satisfaction how willing they were to give him all the security that lay
in there power, they seemed willing to subscribe the two first, as they
stood single, but not to any, if the last must be joyned with them.
But ye Generall used, or urged, a grate many reasons for the signeing
the wholl ingagement, as it was presented in the three conjoyned
branches, other ways no securitye could be expected, neather to the
Countrey, Armye, nor himselfe: therefore he was resalued, if that
they would not do, what hee did judg soe reasonable, and necessary
to be don, in and about the premises, that he would surrender up his
Commission to the Assembley, and let the countrey finde som other
servants to goe abrode and do there worke.

For, sath he, it is to be considered, that Sr William hath allredy Bacons reasons for ye takeing the oath.
proclamed me a Rebell, and it is not unknowne to himselfe that I both
can, and shall charge him with no less then Treason. And it is not
my selfe onely, that must and is concerned in what shall be charged
against him, but severall Gen'amen in the countrey, besides; who
now are, and ever will be against his intress, and of those that shall
adhere to his ilegall proseedings: of which he being more then ord-
narely senceable, it cannot in common reason be otherways conceued,
but that he being assisted by those forces, now implored, that they
shall not be wholly imployed to the destruction of all those capeable
to frame an accuseation against him, to his sacred Majesty. Neather
can it reasonably be apprehended, that he will ever condesend to any
friendly accomadation wth those that shall subscribe to all, or any part
of this ingagement, unless such or such persons shall be surrendred up
to his marcy, to be proseeded against, as he shall thinke fitt: and then

how many, or few, those may be, whom he shall make choyce of, to be
sent into the tother world, that he may be rid of his feares in this, may
be left to consideration.

Many things was (by many of those who were at this meeting)
urged pro and con, concerning the takeing or not takeing of the ingagement: But such was the ressalute temper of the Generall,
against all reasoning to the contrary, that y^r wholl must be swollowed,
or ells no good would be don.   In the urging of which he used such
specious and subtill pretences ; som times for the pressing, and not to
be despenced with necessity, in regarde of those feares the wholl Collony was subjected to through the daly murthers perpetrated by the
Indians, and then againe opening the harmlesness of the Oath, as he
would haue it to be, and which he manidged solely against a grate
many of those counted the wisest men in the Countrey, with so much
art and sophisticall dixterety, that at length there was litle said, by
any. against the same :   Especially when that the Guner of York Fort
arived, imploreing aide to secure the same against the Indians ; adeing
that there was a grate many poore people fled into it for protection,
which could not be, unless there was som speedy course taken to reinforce the said Fort, with Munition and Arms, other ways it, and those
fled to it, would go nere hand to fall in to the power of the Heathen.

The Generall was som what startled at this newes, & accordingly
expostulated the same, how could it posible be that the most coneider-
ablest fortris in the countrey, should be in danger to be surprised by
the Indians.   But being tould that the Governour, the day before, had
caused all the Arms and Amunition to be convayed out of the Fort
into his owne vessell, with which he was saled forth of the Countrey,
as it was thought, it is strange to thinke. what impressions this Story
made upon the peoples apprehentions.   In ernist this action did stager
a grate many, otherways well inclined to Sr William, who could not
tell what constructions to put upon it.   How ever, this was no grate
disadvantage to Bacons designes : he knew well enough how to make
his advantages out of this, as well as he did out of the Gloster busnes,
before mentioned, by frameing and stomping out to the peoples apprehentions what commentaries, or interpretations, he pleased, upon the
least oversight by the Governour commited ; which hee managed with
so much cuning & subtillety, that the peoples minds became quickly
flexable, and apt to receue any impression, or simillitude, that his
Arguments should represent to there ill disarneing judgments ; in so
much that the Oath became now more smooth, and glib, to be swol-

The oath
taken.

lowed, even by those who had the gratest repugnancy against it; so that there was no more descorses used neather for restrictions nor inlargements; onely this salvo was granted, unto those who would clame the benifit of it (and som did soe) yet not exprest in the writen copey (viz.) That if there was any thing in the same of such dangerous consequence that might tant the subscribers Alegence, that then they should stand absalued from all and every part of the s.d oath; unto which the Generall gave his consent (and certainely he had too much cuning to denye, or gaine say it) saying God forbid that it should be other ways ment, or intended; adding that himselfe (and Armye by his command) had, som few days before taken the Oath of Alegience, therefore it could not Rationally be immagined that eather him selfe, or them, would goe about to act, or do, any thing contrary to the meaneing of the same.

Bad Ware requires a darke store, while Sleeke and Pounce inveagles the Chapmans judgment. Though the first subscribers were indulged the liberty of entering there exceptions, against the strict letter of the oath, yet others who were to take the same before the respectiue justices of peace in their severall juridictions, were not to haue y.e same lattitude. For the power of affording cautious, and exceptions, was solely in the imposer, not in those who should here after administer the oath, whereby the aftertakers were obliged to swollow the same (though it might haserd there choakeing) as it stood in the very letter thereoff. Neather can I apprehend what benifit could posible accrew more unto those who were indulged, the fore s.d previllidg, then to those who were debard the same ; since both subscribed the ingagement as it stood in the letter, not as it was in the meaneing of the subscriber. It is trew, before God and there owne conciences, it might be pleadeable, but not at the Bar of humane proseedings, with out a favourable interpretation put upon it, by those who were to be the judges.

While Bacon was contriuing, and imposeing this Illegall Oath, for to secure him selfe against the Governour, the Governour was no less sollicious to finde out meanes to secure him selfe against Bacon. There-fore, as the onely place of securytie, within the Collony, to keep out of Bacons reach, he sales over to Accomack. This place is sequestered from the mane part of Verginia through the enterposition of the grate Bay of Cheispiock, being itselfe an Isthmus, and commonly called the Eastern shore. It is bounded on the East with the maine oacian, and on the Sowth west with the afore s.d Bay, which runs up into the countrey navigable for the bigest Ships more then 240 miles, and so

Sr W. sailes to Acco-mack.

consequently, not approcheable from the other parts of Verginia but by water, without surrounding the head of the s.ᵈ Bay: A labour of toyle, time, and danger, in regard of the way, and habitations of the Indians.

It was not long before Bacon was inform'd where the Governour had taken Santuary; neather was he ignorant what it was that moved him to do what he had don: He did all so apprehend that, as he had

Bland &
Carver sent
to Acco-
mack.

found the way out, he could (when he saw his owne time) finde the way in againe; and though he went forth with an emty hand he might return with a full fist. For the preventing of which (as he thought) he despach'd away one Esqᵗ Bland, a Gen'man of an actiue and stiring dispossition, and no grate admirer of Sᵗ Williams goodness; and with him, in Commission, one Capt. Carver, a person aquainted with Navigation, and one (as they say) indebted to Sᵗ W. (before he dyed) for his life, upon a duble account, with forces in two ships, eather to block Sᵗ William up in Accomack, or other ways to inveagle the inhabitants (thinkeing that all the countrey, like the Friere in the Bush, must needs be soe mad as to dance to there Pipe) to surrender him up in to there hands.

Bacon haueing sent Bland, and the rest, to doe this servis, once

Bacon ad-
vanceth
against the
Indians.

more re-enters upon his Indian march; after that he had taken order for the conveincing an Assembley, to sit downe on the 4 of September, yᵉ Summons being Authentick'd, as they would haue it, under the hands of 4 of the Councell of State; and yᵉ reason of the Convention to manidge the affaires of yᵉ Countrey in his absence; least (as he saide) while hee went abrode to destroy the Wolves, the Foxes, in the meane time, should com and devoure the Sheepe. Hee had not march'd many miles, from his head quarters, but that newes came post hast, that Bland and the rest with him, were snapt at Accomack; betrade (as som of there owne party related) by Capt. Carver: but those who are best able to render an acount of this affaire do aver, that there was no other Treason made use of but there want of discre-

Carver taken
and hanged.

tion, assisted by the juce of the Grape: had it bin other ways the Governour would never rewarded the servis with yᵉ gift of a Halter, which he honoured Carver with, sudenly after his surpriseall. Bland was put in Irons, and ill intreated, as it was saide; most of the soulders owned the Governours cause, by entering them selues in to his servis; those that refused were made prissoners, and promised a releasement at the price of Carvers fate.

The Governour being blest with this good servis, and the better servis, in that it was efected with out blood shed, and being inform'd

that Bacon was entred upon his Indian March, ships him selfe for the Sir W. ships
himselfe for
ye westeru
shore.
western shore, being assisted with 5 ships and 10 sloops, in which (as
it is saide) was about a thousand soulders. The newes where of outstriping his canvis wings soone reach'd the eares of those left by Bacon,
to see the Kings peace kep, by resisting the Kings vice gerent. For
before that the Governour could get over the Water, two fugetiues
was got to land, sent (as may be supposed) from som in Accomack,
spirited for the Generalls quarill, to inform those here, of the same
principles, of the Governours strength, and upon what terms his soulders were to fight. And first they were to be rewarded with those
mens estates who had taken Bacons Oath, catch that catch could.
Secondly that they, and there heirs, for 21 years should be discharged Upon what
terms the
Accomack-
ians were to
fight.
from all impossition, excepting Church dues, and lastly 12 pence per
day, dureing the wholl time of servis. And that it was further decreed
that all Sarvants, whose masters were under the Generall Collours, or
that had subscribed the ingagement, should be set free, and injoy the
fore mention'd benifits, if that they would (in Arms) owne the Governours cause. And that this was the wholl truth, and nothing but the
truth, the two men be fore mention'd, deposed before Capt. Thorp
one of the Iust-asses of the peace, for York County, after that one
Collonell Scarsbrooke had more prudently declined the admiting these
two scoundrills to the test. Whether these flellows were in the right,
or in the rong, as to what they had narated, I know not, but this is certaine, whether the same was trew, or false, it produced the efects of
truth in peoples mindes; who hereby became so much destracted in
there ressalations, that they could not tell, at present, which way to turn The peoples
perplexed
condition..
them selues; while there tongues expresed no other language but what
sounded forth feares, wishes, and execrations, as their apprehentions,
or affections, dictated : All lookeing upon them selues as a people utterly
undon, being equally exposed to the Governours displeasure, and the
Indians blooly cruillties; Som cursing the cause of there approcheing
destruction, lookeing upo the Oath to be no small ingredient, helping
to fill up the measure of there Miserys : Others wishing the Generalls
presence, as there onely Rock of safety, while other look'd upon him
as the onely quick sunds ordnined to swollow up, and sinke the ship
that should set them on shore, or keep them from drownding in the
whirle poole of confuseion.

In the midest of these feares, and perturbations, the Governour Sr W. arives
at Towue,
Sep. 7.
ariues with his Fleet of 5 ships and 10 sloopes, all well man'd (or
appear'd to be soe) before the Towne ; into which the Governour sends

his summons (it being possest by 7 or 800 Baconians) for a Rendition; with a free and ample pardon to all that would decline Bacons intress, and owne his, excepting one Mr. Drummond and one Mr. Larance a Collonell, and both actiue promoters of Bacons designes: Which is a most apparent argument, that what those two men (before mentioned) had sworn to, was a mere pack of untruths. This his Honours Proclamation was acceptable to most in Towne; while others againe would not trust to it, feareing to meet with som after-claps of revenge: Which diverscity of opinions put them all into a ressalution of diserting the place, as not Tenable (but indeed had it bin fortifyed, yet they had no Commission to fight) while they had the liberty of so doeing, before it should be wholly invested; which that night, in the darke, they put in execution, every one shifting for him selfe with no ordnary feare, in the gratest hast posible, for fere of being sent after: And that som of them was posses'd with no ordnary feare, may be manifested in Collonell Larence, whose spirits were so much destracted, at his apprehentions of being one excepted in the Gouernours act of grace, that he forsooke his owne Howse with all his welth and a faire Cupbord of Plate intire standing, which fell into the Governours hands the nex Morning.

The Baconians forsake the towne.

The Towne being thus forsaken, by the Baconians, his Honour enters the same the next day, about noone; where after he had rendred thanks unto God for his safe arivall (which he forgot not to perform upon his knees, at his first footeing the shore) hee applyes himselfe not onely to secure what he had got possesion of, but to increace and inlarge the same to his best advantage. And knowing that the people of ould useally painted the God of war with a belly to be fed, as well as with hands to fight, he began to cast about for the bringing in of provisions for to feed his soulders; and in the next place for soulders, as well to reinforce his strength with in, as to inlarge his quarters abrode: But as the saying is, Man may propose, but God will dispose; when that his hou^r thought him selfe so much at liberty, that he might haue the liberty to go when and where he pleased, his expectations became very speedily & in a moment frusterated.

For Bacon haueing don his buisness against the Indians, or at least so much as he was able to do, haueing marched his men with a grate deale of toyle & haserd som hundreds of miles, one way and another, killing som and takeing others prissoners, and haueing spent his provissions, draws in his forces with in the verge of the English Plantations, from whence he dismiseth the gratest part of his Army to gether strength against the next designed March, which was no sooner don but he incounters the newes of the Governours being arived at town. Of which being informed he with a marvellous cellerity (outstriping the swift wings of fame) marcheth those few men now with him (which hee had onely resarved as a gard to his parson) and in a trice blocks up the Governour in Towne, to the generall astonishment of the wholl Countrey; especially when that Bacons numbers was knowne; which at this time did not exseed aboue a hundred and fifty, and these not above two thirds at worke neather. An action of so strange an Aspect, that who ever tooke notis of it, could not chuse but thinke but that the Accomackians eather intended to receue their promised pay, without disart; or other ways to establish such signall testimonies of there cowerdize or disaffections, or both, that posterity might stand & gaze at there reched stupidety.

Bacon blocks the Governo' up in towne.

Bacon soone perceved what casey worke he was likely to haue, in this servis, and so began to set as small an esteeme upon these mens curages, as they did upon there owne credits. Hee saw, by the Prolog, what sport might be expected in the play, and soe began to dispose of his affaires accordingly. Yet not knowing but that the paucity of his numbers being once knowne, to those in Towne, it might raise there hearts to a degree of curage, haueing so much the ods, and that manitimes number prevales against ressalution, he thought it not amiss, since the Lions strength was too weake, to strengthen the same with the Foxes Braines: and how this was to be efected you shall heare.

For emediately he despacheth two or three parties of Horss, and about so many in each party, for more he could not spare, to bring in to the Camp some of the prime Gent: Women, whose Husbands were in towne. Where when arived he sends one of them to inform her owne, and the others Husbands, for what purposes he had brought them into the camp, namely, to be plac'd in the fore frunt of his Men, at such time as those in towne should sally forth upon him.

Bacon sends for severall Gent: Women in to the camp, and for what.

The poore Gent: Women were mightely astonish'd at this project; neather were there Husbands voide of amazements at this subtill invention. If M' Fuller thought it strange, that the Divells black gard should be enrouled Gods souldiers, they made it no less wonderfull, that there innocent and harmless Wives should thus be entred a white garde to the Divell. This action was a Method, in war, that they were not well aquainted with (no not those the best inform'd in millitary affaires) that before they could com to pearce their enimies sides, they must be obliged to dart there wepons through there wives brest: By which meanes though they (in there owne parsons) might escape without wounds; yet it might be the lamentable fate of there better halfe to drop by gunshott, or other ways be wounded to death.

Whether it was these Considerations, or som others, I do not know, that kep their swords in there scabards: But this is manifest, That Bacon knit more knotts by his owne head in one day, then all the hands in Towne was able to untye in a wholl weeke: While these Ladyes white Aprons became of grater force to keepe the beseiged from salleing out then his works (a pittifull trench) had strength to repell the weakest shot, that should haue bin sent into his Legūre, had he not made use of this invention.

For it is to be noted that rite in his frunt, where he was to lodge his Men, the Governour had planted 3 grate Guns, for to play poynt blank upon his Men, as they were at worke, at about 100 or a 150 paces distance; and then againe, on his right hand, all most close aborde the shore, lay the ships, with ther broade sides, to thunder upon him if he should offer to make an onslaute: this being the onely place, by land, for him to make his entrey, into the Towne: But for your better satisfaction, or rather those who you may show this Naritiue to, who haue neuer bin upon the place, take this short description.

The description of Iames Towne. The place, on which the Towne is built, is a perfict Peninsulla, or tract of Land, all most wholly incompast with Water. Haueing on the Sowth side the River (Formerly Powhetan, now called Iames River) 3 miles brode, Incompast on the North, from the east point, with a deep Creeke, rangeing in a cemicircle, to the west, with in 10 paces of the River; and there, by a smalle Istmos, tacked to ye Continent. This Iseland (for so it is denominate) hath for Longitud (east and west) nere upo 2 miles, and for Lattitude about halfe so much, beareing in the wholl compass about 5 miles, litle more or less. It is low-ground, full of Marches and Swomps, which makes the Aire, especially in ye Sumer, insalubritious & unhelty: It is not at all replenish'd with springs of fresh water, & that which they haue in ther Wells, brackish, ill scented, penurious, and not gratefull to ye stumack; which render the place improper to indure the commencement of a seige. The Towne is built much about the midle of the Sowth line, close upon the River, extending east and west, about 3 quarters of a mile; in which is comprehended som 16 or 18 howses, most as is the Church, built of Brick, faire and large; and in them about a dozen ffamilles (for all the howses are not inhabited) getting there liueings by keepeing of ordnaries, at exstreordnary rates.

The Governour understanding that the Gent: Women, at the Le-
gure, was, by order, drawne out of danger, resalued, if posible, to
beate Bacon out of his trench; which he thought might easely be A salley made upon Bacon.
performed, now that his Gardian Angles had forsaken his Camp.
For the efecting of which he sent forth 7 or (as they say) 800 of
his Accomackians, who (like scholers goeing to schoole) went out with
hevie harts, but returnd hom with light heeles; thinkeing it better
to turne there backs upon that storme, that there brests could not indure to strugle against, for feare of being gauled in there sides, or
other parts of there bodys, through the sharpness of the wether; which
(after a terable noyse of thunder and lightning out of the Easte) began
to blow with a powder (and som leade too as big as musquitt boolitts)
full in there faces, and that with so grate a violence, that som off them
was not able to stand upon there leggs, which made the rest betake
them selues to there heeles; as the onely expedient to save there lives;
which som amongst them had rather to haue lost, then to haue own'd
there safty at the price of such dishonourable rates.

The Governour was exstremly disgusted at the ill management of
this action, which he exprest in som passionate terms, against those
who merited the same. But in ernist, who could expect the event to
be other ways then it was, when at the first notis given, for the designed salley to be put in execution, som of the officers made such
crabed faces at the report of the same, that the Guner of Yorke Fort
did proffer to purchase, for any that would buy, a Collonells, or a Cap-
tains, Commission, for a chunke of a pipe.

The next day Bacon orders 3 grate Guns to be brought into the
Camp, two where of he plants upon his trench. The one he sets to
worke (playing som calls itt, that takes delight to see stately structurs
beated downe, and Men blowne up into the aire like Shutle Cocks)
against the Ships, the other against the enterance into Towne, for to The Govern-our leaves Towne.
open a pasage to his intended Storm, which now was resalued upon as
he said, & which was prevented by the Governours forsakeing the
place, and shiping himselfe, once more to Accomack; takeing along
with him all the Towne people, and there goods, leaveing all the grate
Guns naled up, and the howses emty, for Bacon to enter at his pleas-
ure, and which he did the next morning before day: Where, contrary
to his hopes, he met with nothing that might satisfie eather him selfe
or soulders desires, except few Horsses, two or three sellers of wine,
and som small quantety of Indian Corne with a grate many Tan'd
hides.

The Governour did not presently leaue Iames River, but rested at an Ancor som 20 miles below the Towne, which made Bacon entertaine som thoughts, that eather hee might haue a desire to re-enter his late left quarters, or return and block him up, as he had S⸢ William. And that there was som probabillety S⸢ W. might steare such a course was news from Potomack (a province within the North Verge of Verginia) that Collonell Brent was marching at the head of 1000 Soulders towards Towne in vindication of the Governours quarill. The better to prevent S⸢ Williams designes (if he had a desire to returne) and to hinder his Conjuntion with Brent (after that he had consulted with his Cabinett Councell) he in a most barberous mauer converts yᵉ wholl Towne into flames, cinders and ashes, not so much as spareing the Church, and the first that ever was in Verginia.

Haueing performed this Flagitious, and sacralidgious action (which put the worst of Sperits into a horid Consternation, at so in-humane a fact) he marcheth his men to the Greene spring (the Governours howse soe named) where haueing stade (feasting his Army at the Governours Cost) two or 3 days, till he was inform'd of S⸢ Williams Motion, he wafts his soulders over the River, at Tindells point, in to Glocester County: takeing up his head quarters at Collonell Warners; from whence hee sends out his Mandates, through the wholl County, to give him a Meeting at the Court howse; there to take the ingagement, that was first promoted at the Midle Plantation: for as yet, in this County, it was not admited. While he was seduliously contriveing this affaire, one Cap⸢ Potter arives in post haste from Rapahanock, with news that Coll: Brent was advanceing fast upon him (with a resalution to fight him) at the head of a 1000 men, what horss what foote, if hee durst stay the commencement. Hee had no sooner red the Letter, but hee commands the Drums to beate, for the gathering his soulders under there Collours; which being don hee aquaints them with Brents numbers and resalutions to fight, and then demands theres; which was cherefully answered in the affirmetiue, with showtes and acclemations, while the Drums thunders a March to meet the promised conflict. The Soulders with abundance of cherefullness disburthening them selues of all impediments to expedition, order, and good deciphing, excepting there Oathes, and Wenches: the first where of they retain'd in imitation of there Commanders; the other out of pitty to the poore whores; who seeing so many Men going to kill one another, began to feare that if they staide behinde, for want of doing they might be undon [( ]there being but a few left at hom, excepting ould men, to sett

Bacon sets the Towne on fire.

Goes over into Gloster.

Bacon resalue[s] to fight Brent.

them on worke,) and so chose rather to dye amongst the souldders, then
to be kep from there labour, and so dye for want of excercize. Besides they knew if fortune cast them into there enimys hands, they had
nothing to be plundred of but there honisty; and that, as too grate a
burthen, and not fitt to be worn in a Camp they had left at hom, there-
by to be found the more light, and fit for the servis they were des-
tinated to. And then againe they had heard a pritty good carrecter of
Brent, and they could not tell but that all or most of his Men might be
as good as him selfe; so that let the world go which way it would
(Stand still with Ptollomye, or turne rownd like a whorlegigg with Co-
pernicus) they were likely to com of with a saveing cast, the being
onely to change there Masters, not the trade they were bound pren-
tis to.

Bacon had not marched above 2 or 3 days jurney (and those but
short ones too, as being loth to tire his Laberours before they came to
there worke) but he meets news in post hast, that Brents Men (not *Brents men
souldders) were all run away, and left him to shift for him selfe. For *forsake him.*
they haueing heard that Bacon had beate the Governour out o'th
Towne they began to be afeard (if they should com with in his reach)
that he might beat them out of there lives, and so resalued not to come
nere him. Collonell Brent was mightily astonish'd at the departure of
his followers. saying that they had forsaken the stowtest man, and
ruing'd the fairest estate in Verginia; which was by there cowerdize,
or disaffections, expos'd to the mercy of the Baconians. But they being (as they thought) more obliged to looke after their owne concernes
& lives, then to take notis, eather of his vallour, or estate, or of there
owne Credits, were not to be rought upon by any thing that he could do,
or say; contrary to there owne fancies.

This buisness of Brents haueing (like the hoggs the devill sheard)
produced more noyse then wooll, Bacon, according to the Summons,
meets the Gloster men at the Court howse: where appeard som 6 or 7 *The oath
hundred horss and foot, with there Arms. After that Bacon, in a long *tendred to
Harage, had tendred them the ingagement (which as yet they had not *the Gloster
taken. and now was the onely cause of this Convention) one M.ʳ Cole *Men.*
offered the sence of all the Gloster men, there present: which was
sum'd up in there desires, not to haue the oath imposed upon them, but
to be indulged the benifitt of Neutralitie: But this he would not grant,
telling off them, that in this there request they appear'd like the worst
of sinners, who had a desire to be saved with the righteous, and yet,
would do nothing whereby they might obtaine there salvation; and so

offering to go away, one Coll: Gouge (of his party) calls to him and tould him, that he had onely spoke to the Horss (meaneing the Troopers) and not to the foote. Bacon, in som passion, replide, he had spoke to the Men, and not to the Horss; haueing left that servis for him to do, because one beast best would understand the meaneing of another. And because a minister, one Mr. Wading, did not onely refuse to take the Ingagement, but incouraged others to make him there example, Bacon commited him to the Gard; telling off him that it was his place to Preach in the Church, not in the Camp: In the first he might say what he pleased, but in the last, he was to say no more then what should please him; unless he could fight to better purpose then he could preach.

Mr. Wading, a Minister, imprisson'd.

The Gloster men haueing taken the ingagement, (which they did not till another meeteing, and in another place) and all the worke don on this side the Western Shore, Bacon thought it not a miss, but worth his labour, to go and see how the Accomackians did. It must be confest that he was a Gent:man of a Liberall education, and so consequently must be replenish'd with good maners, which inables, and obligeth all civell parsons both to remember, and repay, receued curtesees: which made him not to forget those kindenesses the Accomackians bestow'd, in his absence, on his friends, and there nighbours, the Verginians: and so now he resalued (since he had nothing ells to do) for to go and repay there kinde hearted vissitt. But first he thought good to send them word of his good meaneing, that they might not pleade want of time, for want of knowledg, to provide a reception answerable to his quallety, and attendance. This was pritty faire play, but really the Accomackians did not halfe like it. They had rather his Hon! would haue had the patience to haue stade till he had bin invited, and then he should haue bin much more wellcom. But this must not hinder his jurnye; if nothing ells enterveine they must be troubled, with a troublesom guest, as well as there neighbours had bin, for a grate while together, to their exstreordnary charge, and utter undoeing. But there kinde, and very mercyfull fate, to whom they, and their Posteritye, must ever remane indebted, observeing there cares and feares, by an admireable, and ever to be cellibrated providence, removed the causes. For

Bacon de-signes to goe to Accomaek.

Bacon haueing for som time, bin beseiged by sickness, and now not able to hould out any longer; all his strength, and provissions being spent, surrendred up that Fort he was no longer able to keepe, into the hands of that grim and all conquering Captaine, Death; after that he

Bacon dyes Octobr 18.

had implor'd the assistance of the above mentioned Minester, for the well makeing his Artickles of Rendition. The onely Religious duty (as they say) he was observ'd to perform dureing these Intregues of affaires, in which be was so considerable an actor, and soe much consearn'd, that rather then he would decline the cause, he be came so deeply ingaged in, in the first rise there of, though much urged by arguments of dehortations, by his nearest Relations and best friends, that he subjected him selfe to all those inconvenences that, singly, might bring a Man of a more Robust frame to his last hom. After he was dead he was bemoned in these following lines (drawne by the Man that waited upon his person, as it is said) and who attended his Corps to there Buriall place : But where depossited till the Generall day, not knowne, onely to those who are ressalutly silent in that particuler. There was many coppes of Verses made after his departure, calculated to the Lattitude of there affections who composed them ; as a rellish taken from both appetites I haue here sent you a cuple.

Bacons Epitaph, made by his Man.

DEATH why soe crewill ! what no other way
To manifest thy splleene, but thus to slay
Our hopes of safety ; liberty, our all
Which, through thy tyrany, with him must fall
To its late Caoss ? Had thy riged force
Bin delt by retale, and not thus in gross
Griefe had bin silent : Now wee must complaine
Since thou, in him, hast more then thousand slane
Whose lives and safetys did so much depend
On him there lif, with him there lives must end.
    If 't be a sin to thinke Death brib'd can bee
Wee must be guilty ; say twas bribery
Guided the fatall shaft. Verginias foes
To whom for secrit crimes, just vengance owes
Disarved plagues, dreding their just disart
Corrupted Death by Parasscelleian art
Him to destroy ; whose well tride curage such,
There heartless harts, nor arms, nor strength could touch.
    Who now must heale those wounds, or stop that blood
The Heathen made, and drew into a flood ?
Who i'st must pleade our Cause ! nor Trump nor Drum
Nor Deputations ; these alass are dumb.
And Cannot speake. Our Arms (though nere so strong)
Will want the aide of his Commanding tongue,
Which Conquer'd more than Ceaser : He orethrew
Onely the outward frame ; this Could subdue

The ruged workes of nature. Soules repleate
With dull Child could, he'd annemate with heate
Drawne forth of reasons Lymbick. In a word
Marss and *Minerva*, both in him Concurd
For arts, for arms, whose pen and sword alike
As *Catos* did, may admireation strike
In to his foes; while they confess with all
It was there guilt stil'd him a Criminall.
Onely this differance doth from truth proceed
They in the guilt, he in the name must bleed
While none shall dare his *Obseques* to sing
In disarv'd measures; untill time shall bring
Truth Crown'd wth freedom, and from danger free
To sound his praises to posterity.

   Here let him rest; while wee this truth report
Hee's gon from hence unto a higher Court
To pleade his Cause: where he by this doth know
WHETHER TO CEASER HEE WAS FRIEND, OR FOE.

Vpon the Death of G: B.

   WHETHER to Ceaser he was Friend or Foe?
Pox take such Ignorance, do you not know?
Can he be Friend to Ceaser, that shall bring
The Arms of Hell, to fight againt the King?
(Treason, Rebellion) then what reason haue
Wee for to waite upon him to his Grave,
There to express our passions? Wilt not bee
Worss then his Crimes, to sing his Ellegie
In well tun'd numbers; where each Ella beares
('To his Flagitious name) a flood of teares?
A name that hath more soules with sorow fed,
Then reched Niobe, single teares ere shed;
A name that fil'd all hearts, all eares, with paine,
Untill blest fate proclamed, Death had him slane.
Then how can it be counted for a sin
Though Death (nay though my selfe) had bribed bin,
To guide the fatall shaft? we honour all
That lends a hand unto a T[r]ators fall.
What though the well paide Rochit soundly ply
And box the Pulpitt, in to flatterey;
Urging his Rethorick, and straind elloquence,
T' adorne incoffin'd filth and excrements;
Though the Defunct (like ours) nere tride
A well intended deed untill he dide?
'Twill be nor sin, nor shame, for us, to say
A two fould Passion checker-workes this day

Of Ioy and Sorow ; yet the last doth move
On feete impotent, wanting strength to prove
(Nor can the art of Logick yeild releife)
How Ioy should be surmounted, by our greife.
Yet that wee Gฤve it cannot be denide,
But 'tis because he was, not cause he dide.
So wep the poore destresed, Ilynm Dames
Hereing those nam'd, there Citty put in flames,
And Country rning'd ; If wee thus lament
It is against our present Ioyes consent.
For if the rule, in Phisick, trew doth prove,
Remove the cause, th' effects will after move,
We haue outliv'd our sorows ; since we see
The Causes shifting, of our miserey.
    Nor is't a single cause, that's slipt away,
That made us warble out, a well-a-day.
The Braines to plot, the hands to execute
Projected ills, Death Ioyntly did nonsute
At his black Bar. And what no Baile could save
He hath commited Prissoner to the Grave ;
From whence there's no repreive. Death keep him close
We haue too many Divells still goe loose.

Ingrams Proceedings.

The Lion had no sooner made his exitt, but the Ape (by indubitable right) steps upon the stage. Bacon was no sooner removed by the hand of good providence, but another steps in, by the wheele of fickle fortune. The Countrey had, for som time, bin guided by a company of knaves, now it was to try how it would behave it selfe under a foole. Bacon had not long bin dead, (though it was a long time be fore som would beleive that he was dead) but one Ingram (or Isgrum, which you will) takes up Bacons Commission (or ells by the patterne of that cuts him out a new one) and as though he had bin his natureall heire, or that Bacons Commission had bin granted not onely to him selfe, but to his Executors, Administraters and Assignes, he (in the Millitary Court) takes out a Probit of Bacons will, and proclames him selfe his Successer.

This Ingram, when that he came first into the Countrey, had gott upon his Back the title of an Esquire. but how he came by it may pussell all the Herolds in England to finde out, u[n]till he informs them of his right name : how ever, by the helpe of this (and his fine capering, for it is saide that he could dance well upon a Rope) he caper'd him

Ingram takes up Bacons Commission.

selfe in to a fine (though short liv'd) estate: by marying, here, with a rich Widow, vallued at som hundreds of pounds.

The first thing that this fine fellow did, after that he was mounted upon the back of his Commission, was to Spur, or Switch, those who were to pay obedience unto his Authorety, by geting him selfe proclaimed Generall of all the forces, now raised, or here after to be raised, in Verginia: Which while it was performing at the head of the Army, the Milke-sop stoode with his hatt in his hand, lookeing as demurely as the grate Turks Muftie, at ye readeing som holy sentance, extracted forth of the Alchron. The Bell-man haueing don, he put on his hat, and his Iannessarys threw up there Caps; crying out as lowde as they could Bellow, God save our new Generall, hopeing, no dout, but he, in imitation of the grat Sultaine, at his election, would haue inlarged there pay, or ells haue given them leave to haue made Iewes of ye best Christians in the Countrey: but he being more than halfe a jew him self, at present forbad all plundrings, but such as he him selfe should be parsonally at.

It was not long before the Governour (still at Accomack) had intimation of Bacons death. He had a long time bin shut up in the Arke (as we may say) and now thought good to send out a winged Messinger to see, if happely, ye Delluge was any whit abated; and whether any dry-ground emerg'd its head, on which, with safety, he might sett his foot, without danger of being wetshod in blood, which accordingly he effected, under the command of one Mā Beverly: a parson calculated to the Lattitude of the Servis, which required descretion, Cūrage, & Celerity, as qualetys wholly subservaut to millitary affares: And all though he returnd not with an Olive branch in his Mouth, the Hyrogliph of peace. yet he went back with the Laurell upon his browes, the emblim of Conquest and tryumph, haueing snapt up one Coll: Hansford, and his party, who kep garde, at the Howse where Coll: Reade did once live. It is saide that Hansford, at (or a litle before) the onslaut, had forsaken the Capitole of Marss, to pay his oblations in the Temple of Venus; which made him the easēre preay to his enimies; but this I haue onely upon report, and must not aver it upon my historicall reputation: But if it was soe, it was the last Sacrylize he ever after offred at the Shrine of that Luxurious Diety, for presently after that he came to Accomack, he had the ill luck to be the first Verginian borne that dyed upon a paire of Gallows. When that he came to the place of Execution (which was about a Mile removed from his prisson) he seemed very well resalued to undergo the utmost mallize

Proclaimed Generall.

Beverly takes Hansford

of his not over kinde Destinie, onely Complaineing of the maner of his death: Being obserued neather at the time of his tryall (which was by a Court Martiall) nor afterwards, to suplicate any other faviour, then that he might be shot like a Soulder, and not to be hang'd like a Dog. But it was tould him, that what he so passionately petitioned for could not be granted, in that he was not condem'd as he was merely a Soulder, but as a Rebell, taken in Arms against the King, whose Laws had ordaind him that death. Dureing the short time he had to live, after his sentance, he approved to his best advantage for the well fare of his soule, by repentance and contrition for all his Sinns, in generall, excepting his Rebelellion, which he would not acknowledg; desireing the People, at the place of execution, to take notis that he dyed a Loyall Subject, and a lover of his Countrey; and that he had never taken up arms, but for the destruction of the Indians, who had murthered so many Christians.

Hansford Executed.

The buisness being so well accompish'd, by those who had taken Hansford, did so raise there Spirits, that they had no sooner deliver'd there Fraight, at Accomack, but they hoyse up there sailes, and back againe to Yorke River, where with a Marvellous celerity they surprise one Major Cheise-Man, and som others, amongst whom one Capt Wilford, who (it is saide) in the bickering lost one of his eyes, which he seem'd litle concern'd at, as knowing, that when he came to Accomack, that though he had bin stark blinde, yet the Governour would take care for to afford him a guide, that should show him the way to the Gallows. Since he had promised him a hanging, long before, as being one of those that went out with Bacon, in his first expedition against the Indians, without a Commission.

Cheiseman and Wilford surpri[sed] by Beverly.

This Capt Wilford, though he was but a litle man, yet he had a grate heart, and was knowne to be no Coward. He had for som yeares bin an Interpreter betwene the English and the Indians, in whose affaires he was well aquainted, which rendred him the more acceptable to Bacon, who made use of him all along in his Indian War. By birth he was the Second Son of a Kt, who had lost life and estate in the late Kings quarill, against the surnamed long Parliament, which forst him to Verginia (the onely Citty of Refuge left in his Majesties dominians, in those times, for destresed Cavallers) to seeke his fortunes, which through his industerey began to be considerable, if the kindness of his fate had bin more perminent, and not destin'd his life to so reched a death. Major Cheisman, before he came to his triall, dyed in prisson, of feare, Greife, or bad useage, for all these are

Cheiseman dies in prisson.

reported: and so by one death prevented another more dredfull to flesh and blood.

There is one remarkeable passage reported of this Major Cheismans Lady, which because it sounds to the honour of her Sex, and consequent[l]y of all loveing Wives, I will not deny it a roome in this Narratiue.

M.̱ Cheismans grate affections for her husband. When that the Major was brought in to the Governor' presence, and by him demanded, what made him to ingage in Bacons designes? Before that the Major could frame an Answer, to the Governours demand; his Wife steps in and tould his hon.̱ that it was her provocations that made her Husband joyne in the Cause that Bacon contended for; ading, that if he had not bin influenc'd by her instigations, he had never don that which he had don. Therefore (upon her bended knees) A kinde Wife. she desired of his hon.̱ that since what her Husband had don, was by her meanes, and so, by Consequence, she most guilty, that shee might be hang'd, and he pardon'd. Though the Governouer did know, that what she had saide, was neare to the truth, yet he saide litle to her request, onely telling of her that she was a W——. But his hon.̱ was angrey, & therefore this expression must be interprited the efeets of his passion, not his meaneing: For it is to be understood in reason, that there is not any Woman, who hath soe small affection, for her Husband, as to dishonour him by her dishonisty, and yet retaine such a degree of love, that rather then he should be hang'd, shee will be content to submit her owne life to the Sentance, to keep her husband from y° Gallows.

Cap.̱ Farlow executed. Cap.̱ Carver & Capt. Farlow was now (or about this time) Executed, as is before hinted. Farlow was related to Cheisman, as he had maried Farlows Neice. When that he went first into the servis (which was presently after that Bacon had receued his Commission) he was Chosen Commander of those recrutes sent out of Yorke County, to Make up Bacons Numbers, according to the Gage of his Commission, limited for the Indian Servis; and by S.̱ William (or som one of the Councell) recommended to Bacon, as a fitt parson to be Commander of the saide party. These terms, by which he became ingaged, under Bacons Commands, he urged in his pley, at his triall: Ading, that if he had, in what he had don, denyed the Generalls orders, it was in his power to hang him, by the judgment of a Court Martiall; and that he had acted nothing but in obedience to the Generalls Authority. But it was replide, against him, that he was put under Bacons command for the servis of the Countrey, against the Indians, which imploy he ought to haue kep to, and not to haue acted by yond his bounds, as he had don: And Since he went into the Army under the Governours orders, he was required to Search the Same, and see if he could finde one that Commissionated him to take up Arms in oppossition to the Governours Authority and parson: Neather had Bacon any other power, by his Commission (had the same bin never so legally obtained) but onely to make war upon the Indians. Farlow rejoyned, that Bacon was, by his Commission, to see that the Kings peace was kep, and to Suppress those that should indeviour to Perturbe the same. It was reply'd, this might be granted him, and he might make his advantage of it, but was required to consider, whether the Kings peace was to be kep in resisting the Kings emediate Governour, soe as to levy a War against him; and so commanded him to be silent, while his sentance was pronounced. This man was much pittied by those who were aquainted with him, as one of a peaceable dispossition, and a good scholer, which one might thinke should haue inabled him to have taken a better estimate of his imployment, as he was äquainted with the Mathamaticks: But it seems the Asstrolabe, or Quadrant, are not the fitest instruments to take the altitude of a Subjects duty; the same being better demonstrated by practicall, not Speculatiue observations.

The nimble, and timely servis, performed by Major Beverly (before mentioned) haueing opened the way, in som measure, the Governour once more sallyeth out for the Westerne Shore, there to make triall of his better fortune; which now began to cast a more favourable Aspect upon him and his affaires; by removeing the maine obstickles out of the way, by a Death, eather Natureall, or violent, (the one the ordnary, the other the exstreordnary workings of providence) which had with such pertinances, and violent perstringes, aposed his most Auspicious proceedings. The last time he came, he made choyce of Iames River; now he was resalued to set up his Rest in Yorke, as haueing the nearest Vicinety to Gloster County (the River onely enterposeing betwene it and Yorke) in which, though the Enimy was the strongest (as desireing to make it the Seate of the Warr, in regard of severall locall covenencies) yet in it he knew that his friends was not the weakest, whether wee respect number, or furniture. It is trew they had taken the ingagement (as the rest had) to Bacon: but hee being dead, and the ingagement being onely personall, was lade in the Grave with him; for it was not made to him selfe, his heires, Executors, administrater, and Assignes; if other ways, it might haue bin

Sr Will. removes to Yorke River.

induced with a kinde of immortallety; unless the Sword, or juster (or
grater) power might hapen to wound it to death. But, how ever
Bacon being Dead, and with him his Commission, all those, who had
taken the ingagement, were now at liberty to go and chuse them selues
another Master.

But though his hon? knew that though they were discharged from
the bindeing power of the oath, yet they were not free from the Commanding power of those Men that was still in Arms, in persuance of
those ends for which the ingagement was pretended to be taken : And
that before this could be effected, those Men must first be beaten from
there Arms, before the other could get there heeles at liberty, to do him
any servis. Therefore he began to cast about how he might remove
those Blocks which stoode in the Gloster Mens way : which being
once don, it must take away all Pretences, and leave them with out all
excuse, if they should offer to sitt still, when he, and his good providence together, had not onely knock'd off there shackles, but eather
imprisson'd there Iaylers, or tide them up to the Gallows.

The strength
Sr Will.
had, at his
coming to
York.
He had with him now in Yorke River 4 Shipps besides 2 or 3
Sloopes. Three of the Ships he brought with him from Accomack : the
other (a Marchantman, as the rest were) was som time before arived
out of England, and in these about 150 Men, at his emediate command ; and no more he had when he came into Yorke River : Where
being setled in Consultation with his friends, for the Manageing of his
affaires, to the best advantage ; he was informed that there was a party
of the Baconians (for so they were still denominated, on that side, for
destinction sake) that had setled them selues in there winter quarters,
at the howse of one Mr Howards, in Gloster county.

For to keepe these Vermin from breeding, in there warme Kenill,
he thought good, in time, for to get them ferited out. For the accom-
plishment of which peice of servis, he very secritly despacheth away
Beverly sur-
priseth Coll:
Harris in
Gloster.
a select number under the Conduct of Major Beverly, who very nimbly
performed the same, haueing the good fortune (as it is saide) to catch
them all a sleepe. And least the Good man of ye Howse should for-
gett this good servis, that Beverly had don him, in removeing his (to
him) chargable guess, with these sleepers, he convayes a good quantety of there Landlords goods aborde : the Baconians (where of one a
Leif? Collonell) to remane prissoners, and the goods to be devided
amongst those whose servis had made them such, according to the Law
of Arms; which Howard will haue to be the Law of HARMS, by
placeing the first letter of his name before the vowill A.

But in ernist (and to leave jesting) Howard did really thinke it hard measure, to see that go out of his store, by the Sword, which he intended to deliver out by the Ell, or yard. Neather could his Wife halfe like the Markitt; when she saw the Chapmen carey her Daughters Husband away Prissoner, and her owne fine Cloathes goeing into Captivity: to be sould by Match and pin; and after worne by those who (before these times) was not worth a point; Yet it is thought, that the ould Gent: Woman, was not so much concern'd that her Son in Law was made a prissoner, as her Daughter was vext, to see they had not left one Man upon the Plantation, to comfort, neather herself nor Mother.

This Block (and no less was the Commander of the fore mention'd sleepers) being removed out of the way, the Gloster Men began to stir abrode: Not provoked thereto out of any hopes of geting, but through a feare of loseing. They did plainely perceue that if they them selues did not goe to worke, sombody ells would, while they (for there neglegence) might be compeld to pay them there wages; and what that might com to they could not tell, since it was probable, in such Servises, the Laberours would be there owne Carvers; and it is commonly knowne, that Soulders makes no Conscience to take more then there due. *The Gloster men rise for Sr W.*

The worke that was now to be don. in these parts (and further I cannot go for want of a guide) was cut out into severall parcells, according as the Baconians had devided the same. And first At Wests Point (an Isthmos which gives the Denomination to the two Rivers, Pomunkey and Mattapony (Indian Names) that branch forth of York River, Som 30 Miles above Tindells point) there was planted a garde of about 200 Soulders. This place Bacon had designed to make his prime Randevouze, or place of Retreat, in respect of severall locall Conveuencis, this place admited off, and which hee found fitt for his purpose, for sundry reasons. Here it was, I thinke, that Ingram did cheifely reside, and from whence he drew his recruts, of Men and Munition. The next Parcell, considerable, was at Green-spring (the Governours howse) into which was put about 100 Men, and Boys, under the Command of on Cap! Drew; who was ressalutely bent (as he sade) to keep the place in spite of all opposition, and that he might the better keepe his promise he caused all the Avenues, and approaches to the same, to be Baracado'd up, and 3 grate Guns planted to beate of the Assalents. A third parcell (of about 30 or 40) was put in to the Howse of Collonell Nath: Bacons (a Gent: Man related to him deceased, *What soulders at West Point. At Greene Spring. At Coll. Bacon's.*

but not of his principles) under the Command of one Major Whaly, a
stout ignorant Fellow (as most of the rest) as may be seene here after;
these were the most considerablest parteys that the Gloster Men were
to deale with, and which they had promised to reduce to obediance, or
other ways to beate them out of there lives, as som of them (perhaps
not well aquainted with Millitary affairs, or too well conseated of there
owne vallour) bosted to doe.

The Parson that, by Commission, was to perform this worke, was
one Major Lawrence Smith (and for this servis so intitled, as it is
saide) a Gent: Man that in his time had hued out many a knotty peice
of worke, and soe the better knew how to handle such ruged fellowes
as the Baconians were famed to be.

The place for him to Congregate his men at (I say Congregate, as
a word not improper, since his second, in dignity, was a Minester, who
had lade downe the Miter and taken up the Helmett) was at one Major
Pates (in whose Howse Bacon had surrendred up both Life and Commission; the one to him that gaue it, the other to him that tooke it)
where there apeared men enuough to haue beaten all the Rebells in the
Countrey, onely with there Axes and Hoes, had they bin led on by a
good overseer.

The proper-
ties of a good
Generall.
I haue eather heard, or haue read, That a Compleate Generall
ought to be owner of these 3 induments: Wisdom to foresee. Experience to chuse, and Curage to execute. He that wants the 2 last, can
never haue the first; since a wise Man will never undertake more
then he is able to perform; He that hath the 2 first, wanting the last,
makes but a lame Commander; since Curage is an inseperable Adjunct
to the bare name of a Souldier, much more to a Generall: He that
wants the second, haueing the first & the last, is no less imperflet then
the other; since without experience, wisdom and curage (like yong
Docters) do but grope in the darke, or strike by gess.

A riseing in
Midlesex.

Walklet
sent to sup-
press it.

Smith
marches af-
ter Walklett.
Much about the time that the Gloster Men Mustred at M. Pates,
there was a riseing in Midle sex, upon the same acount: Who were no
sooner gott upon ther feet, but yᵉ Baconians resalues to bring them
on there knees. For the efecting of which Ingram speeds away one
Walklett, his Leif: Generall, (a Man much like the Master) with a
party of Horss, to do the worke. M. L. Smith was quickly inform'd
upon what arend Walklett was sent, and so, with a Generous ressalution, resalues to be at his heeles, if not before hand with him, to helpe
his friends in there destress. And because he would not all together
trust to others, in affaires of this nature, he advanceth at the head of

his owne Troops, (what Horss what Foote for number, is not in my intillegence) leaveing the rest for to fortify Major Pates howse, & so speeds after Walklet who, before Smith could reach the required distance, had performed his Worke, with litle labour, and (hereing of Smiths advance) was prepareing to giue him a Reception answerable to his designements: Swareing to fight him though Smith should out number him Cent per cent; and was not this a darcing ressalution of a Boy that hardly ever saw Sword, but in a Scaberd?

In the meane time that this buisnes was a doeing, Ingram understanding upon what designe M. L. Smith was gon about, by the advice of his officers strikes in betwene him and his new made (and new mand) Garisson at M. Pates. He very nimbly invests the Howse, and then summons the Soulders (then under the command of the fore said Minester) to a speedy rendition, or otherways to stand out to Mercy, at there utmost perill. After som toos and froes about the buisness (quite beyond his text) the Minester accepts of Such Articles, for a Surrender, as pleased Ingram, and his Mermidons, to grant.

Ingram takes the Gloster Men at M. Pates.

Ingram had no sooner don this jobb of jurnye worke (of which he was not a litle proud) but M. L. Smith (haueing retracted his March out of Midle-sex, as thinkeing it litle less then a disparagement to haue any thing to doe with Walklett) was up on the back of Ingram, before he was aware, and at which he was not a litle daunted, feareing that he had beate Walklett to peices, in Midlesex. But he perceueing that the Gloster Men did not weare (in there faces) the Countinances of Conquerers, nor there Cloathes the marks of any late ingagement (being free from the honourable Staines of Wounds and Gun shott) he began to hope the best, and the Gloster men to feare the worst; and what the properties of feare is, let Feltham tell you, who saith, That if curage be a good Oriter, feare is a bad Counceller, and a worss Ingineare. For insteade of erecting, it boutes and batters downe all Bullworks of defence: perswadeing the feeble hart that there is no safety in armed Troops, Iron gates, nor stone walls. In oppossition of which Passion I will appose the Properties of it's Antithesis, and say That as som men are never vallent but in the midst of discourse, so others never manifest there Courage but in the midst of danger: Never more alive then when In the jawes of Death, crowded up in the midst of fire, smoke, Swords and gunns; and then not so much laying about them through desparcation, or to saue there lives, as through a Generosety of Spirit, to trample upon the lives of there enimies.

M. G. Smith retracts his March from Walklett.

For the saveing of Pouder and Shott (or rather through the before

Major Bris-
tow chall: to
Ingram.

mentioned Generossety of Curage) one Major Bristow (on Smiths side) made a Motion to try the equity, and justness of the quarill, by single Combett: Bristow proffering him selfe against any one (being a Gen!) on the other side; this was noble, and like a Soulder. This Motion (or rather Challenge) was as redely accepted by Ingram, as proffer'd by Bristow; Ingram Swareing, the newest Oath in fashion, that he would be the Man ; and so advanceth on foot, with sword and Pistell, against Bristow; but was fetch'd back by his owne men, as douteing the justness of there cause, or in Consideration of the desparety that was betwene the two Antagonist. For though it might be granted, that in a private Condition, Bristow was the better man, yet now it was not to be alowed, as Ingram was intitled.

This buisness not fadging, betwene the two Champions, the Gloster men began to entertaine strange, and new Ressalutions, quite Retrogade to there pretentions, and what was by all goodmen expected from the promiseing asspects of this there Leagueing against a usurping power. It is saide that a good Cause and a good Deputation, is a lawfull Authorety for any Man to fight by ; yet neather of these, joyntly nor Severally, hath a Coercive power, to make a Man a good Soulder: If he wants Courage, though he is inlisted under both, yet is he not

The Gloster
men submitt
to Ingram.

starling quoyne : he is at best but Coper, stompt with the Kings impress, and will pass for no more then his just vallew. As to a good Cause, doutless, they had Satisfied themselves as to that, ells what were they at this time a Contending for, and for whom? And as for a good Deputation, if they wanted that, where fore did they so miserably befoole them selves, as to run in to the mouths of there enimies, and there to stand still like a Company of Sheep, with the knife at there throtes, and never so much as offer to Bleat ; for the saving of there lives, liberties, Estates, and what to truly vallient men is of grater vallew then these, there Creditts? all which now lay at the Mercy of there enimies, by a tame surrender of there Arms, and Parsons in to the hands of Ingram (with out Strikeing one Stroke) who haueing made all the cheife Men prissoners (excepting those who first run away) he dismist the rest to there owne abodes, there to Sum up the number of those that were eather slane or wounded, in this Servis.

Farrill at-
temps the
Baconians
under
Whaly's
Command.

Much about this time, of the Gloster buisness, his hon' sends abrode a party of Men, from off aboarde, under the Command of one Hubert Farrill, to fferitt out a Company of the Rebells, who kep Gard at Coll. Bacons, under the power of Major Whaly, before mentioned. Coll.

Bacon himselfe, and one Coll: Ludwell, came along with Farrill, to see
to the Management of the enterprise ; about which they tooke all posible care, that it might prove fortunate.   For they had no sooner resalued upon the onsett, but they consult on the Maner, which was to be
effected by a Generossety paralell with the designe ; which required
Curage, and expedition : and so concludes not to answer the Centreys
by fireing ; but to take, kill, or drive them up to there Avenues, and
then to enter pell mell with them in to the howse : this Method was
good had it bin as well executed, as Contrived.   But the Centrey had
no sooner made the Challinge, with his mouth, demanding who Coms
there ? but the other answer with there Musquits (which seldom
Speakes the language of friends) and that in soe loud a Maner, that it
alarum'd those in the howse to a defence, and then in to a posture to
salley out.   Which the other perceueing (contrary to there first orders)
wheeles of from the danger, to find a place for there securytie, which
they in part found, behinde som out buildings, and from whence they
fired one upon the other, giueing the Bullits leave to grope there owne
way in the dark (for as yet it was not day) till the Generall was shot
through his loynes ; and in his fate all the soulders (or the grater part)
through there hearts, Now sunke in to there heels which they were now
makeing use of instead of there hands, the better to saue there jackits,
of which they had bin Certainely Stript, had they Com under there
enimies fingers, who knowes better how to Steale then fight, not with- ^{Farrill kild.}
standing this uneven Cast of Fortunes Mallize.   Being a Conflict, in
which the losers haue cause to repent, and the winers Faith to giue
God thanks ; unless with the same devotion Theives do when that they
haue stript honist Men out of there Mony.   Here was none but there
Generall kild, whose Commission was found droping-wett with his owne
blood, in his pockitt ; and 3 or 4 taken prisoners ; what wounded not
knowne, if any, in there backs ; as there enimies say ; who glory'd more
in there Conquest then ever Scanderbeg did, for the gratest victory he
ever obtained against the Turkes.   If Sr Williams Cause were no better then his fortunes, hither to, how many prossellites might his disas-
ters bring over to the tother side ? but God forbid that the justice of
all quarills should be estimated by there events.

     Yet here in this action (as well as som other before) who can chuse
but deplore the strange fate that the Governour was subjected to, in
the evill choyce of his cheife-commanders, for the leadeing on his Millitary transactions ; that when his cause should com to a day of heareing, they should want Curage to put in there pleay of defence, against

there Adverssarys arguments; and pittyfully to stand still and see
themselues nonsuted, in every sneakeing adventure, or Action, that cal'd
upon there Generossety, (if they had had any) to vindicate there indubitable pretences against a usurped power.

It is trew Whalys Condition was desperate, and hee was resalved
that his Curage should be conformable & as desperate as his Condition.
He did not want intilligence how Hansford, and Som others, was sarved
at Accomack; which made him thinke it a grate deale better to dye
like a Man, then to be hang'd like a Dogg; if that his Fate would but
give him the liberty of picking as well as he had taken the liberty of
stealeing; of which unsoulder-like quallety he was fowly guilty. But
let Whaleys condition be never so desperate, and that he was resalud
to Manage an oppossition against his Assalent according to his condition, yet those in the Howse with him stoode upon other terms, being
two thirds (and the wholl exsceeded not 40) prest into the Servis, much
against there will; and had a grater antipethy against Whaly then they
had any cause for to feare his fate, if he, and they too, had bin taken.
As for that Objection, that Farrill was not, at this time, fully cūred of
those Wounds he receved in the Salley at Towne, which in this action
proved detrimentall both to his strength and curage: Why then (if it
was so) did he accept of this imploy (he haueing the liberty of refuseing) since none could be better aquainted with his owne Condition
(eather for strength or Courage) better then him selfe? Certainely in
this particuler, Farills foolish ostentation was not excuseable, nor Sᵗ
William with out blame, to Complye with his ambition, as he had no
other parts to prove himselfe a Soulder, then a haire brain'd ressalution to put him selfe forward in those affaires he had no more aquaintance with then what he had heard people talke off; For the falure of
this enterprise (which must wholly be refer'd to the breach he made
upon their sedulōus determinations) which was (as is intimated before,
to croude in to the Howse with the Centrey) was not onely injurious
to there owne party, by leting slip so faire an occasion, to weaken the
power of the enimy, by removeing Whaly out of the way, who was
esteemed the Most Considerablest parson on that side; but it was, and
did prove of bad cosequence to the adjacent parts, where he kep gard:
For where as before he did onely take ame where he might do mischeife, he now did mischeife with out takeing ame: before this unhapic
conflict, he did levie at this, or that particuler onely, but now he shott

Ingram
reduced by
Grantham.

at Rovers, let the same lite where it would he matter'd nott.

Cap': Grantham had, now, bin som time in Yorke River. A man unto whom Verginia is very much beholden for his neate contrivance in bringing Ingram (and som others) over to harken to reason. With Ingram he had som small aquaintance, for it was in his Ship that he came to Verginia; and so resalued to try if he might not doe that by words, which others could not accomplish wth Swords. Now all though he knew that Ingram was the Point, where all the lines of his contrivance were for to Center, yet he could not tell, very well, how to obtaine this point. For all though he did know that Ingram, in his private Condition, was accostable enough; yet since the Tit Mouse (by one of Fortunes figaryes) was becom an Elliphant, he did not know but that his pride, might be as immence as his power: since the Peacock (though bred upon a Dung-hill) is no less proud of his fine fethers then the princely Eagle is of his noble curage. What Arguments Grantham made use of, to ring the Sword out of Ingrams hand, to me is not visable, more then what he tould me of; which I thinke was not Mercuriall enough, against an ordnary Sophester. But to speake the truth, it may be imagin'd that Grantham (at this time) could not bring more reasons to Convince Ingram, then Ingram had in his owne head to Convince him selfe; and so did onely a wate som favourable overtures (and such as Grantham might, it is posible, now make) to bring him over to the tother side. Neather could he apprehend more reason in Granthams Arguments, then in his owne affaires, which now provok'd him to dismount from the back of that Horss which he wanted skill. and strength, to Manidge; especially there being som, of his owne party, wateing an opertunity to toss him out of the Sadle, of his new mounted honours; and of whose designes he wanted not som intilligence, in the Countinances of his Mermidons; who began for to looke a skew upon this, there Milk-sopp Generall; who they judged fitter to dance upon a Rope, or in som of his wenches lapps, then to caper, eather to Bellonies Bagpipe, or Marssos whisle.

But though Ingram was won upon, to turn honist, in this thing (thanks to his necessitye, which made it an act of Compultion, not a free will offering) yet was the worke but halfe don, untill the Soulders were wrought upon to follow his example. And though he him selfe, or any body clls, might command them to take up there Arms, when any mischeife was to be don: yet it was a question whether he, or any in the Countrye, could command them to lay downe there Arms, for to efect or do any good. In such a case as this, where Authority wants power, descretion must be made use of, as a vertue Surmounting a brutish force. Grantham, though he had bin but a while in the Coun-

trey, and had scene but litle, as to mater of Action, yet he had heard a
grate deale ; and So Much that the name of Authority had but litle
power to ring yᵉ Sword out of these Mad fellows hands, as he did
perceue.   And that there was more hopes to efect that by smoothe
words, which was never likely to be accomplish'd by rough deeds ;
there fore he resalued to accoste them, as the Divell courted Eve,
though to a better purpose, with never to be performed promises :
counting it no sin to Ludificate those for there good, that had bin de-
ceued by others to there hurt.   He knew that Men were to be treated
as such, and Children according to there childish dispossitions : And
all though it was not with both these he was now to deale, yet he was
to observe the severall tempers of those he was to worke upon.

Grantham at
West Point.   What number of Soulders was, at this time, in Garrisson at West
Point, I am not Certane : It is saide about 250, sum'd up in freemen,
scarvants and slaues ; these three ingredience being the Compossition
of Bacons Army, ever since that the Governour left Towne.   These
was informed (to prepare the way) two or three days before that Grantham came to them, that there was a treaty on foote betweue there
Generall, and the Governour ; and that Grantham did manely promote
the same, as he was a parson that favoured the cause, that they were
contending for.

When that Grantham arived, amongst these fine fellowes, he was
receued with more then an ordnary respect ; which he haueing repade,
with a suteable deportment, he aquaints them with his Commission,
which was to tell them, that there was a peace Concluded betwene yᵉ
Governour and there Generall ; aū since him self had (in som meas-
Upon what
terms West-
Point was
surrendred.   ures) used his indeviours, to bring the same to pass, hee beg'd of the
Governour, that he might haue the hon⸗ to com and aquaint them
with the terms ; which he saide was such, that they had all cause to
rejoyce at, then any ways to thinke hardly of the same ; there being a
Compleate satisfaction to be given (by the Articles of agreement) according to every ones particuler intress ; which he sum'd up under
these heads.   And first, those that were now in Arms (and free Men)
under the Generall, were still to be retained in Arms, if they so
pleased, against the Indians.   Secondly, And for those who had a desire
for to return hom, to there owne abodes, care was taken for to haue
them satisfide, for the time they had bin out, according to the alowance
made the last Assembley.   And lastly, those that were sarvants in Arms,
and behaued them selues well, in there imployment, should emediately
receve discharges from there Indentures, signed by the Governour, or

Sequetary of State; and there Masters to receue, from the publick, a valluable Satisfaction, for every Sarvant, so set free (Marke the words) proportionally to the time that they haue to serve.

Upon these terms, the Soulders forsake West-Point, and goe with Grantham to kiss the Governours hands (still at Tindells point) and to receue the benifitt of the Articles mentioned by Grantham; where when they came (which was by water, them selues in one vessill, and there Arms in another; and so contrived by Grantham, as he tould me him selfe, upon good reason) the Sarvants and Slaves was sent hom to there Masters, there to stay till the Governour had leasure to signe there discharges; or to say better, till they were free, according to the Custom of the Countrey, the rest was made prissoners, or entertain'd by the Governour, as hee found them inclin'd.

Of all the obstickles, that hath, hither to, lane in the Governours way, there is not one (which hath falne with in the Verge of my intilligence) that hath bin removed by the Sword; excepting what was performed under the Conduct of Beverly: How this, undertaken by Grantham, was effected, you haue heard; though badly (as the rest) by me Sum'd up. The next, that is taken notis of, is that at Greene Spring (before hinted) under the Command of one Cap! Drew, formerly a Miller (by profession) though now Dignifide with the title of a Cap! ꞏꞏꞏꞏꞏꞏꞏꞏ erly beholden unto S! William; and soe, by way of requiteall, most likely to keepe him out of his owne Howse. This Whisker of Whorly-Giggs, perceueing (now) that there was More Water coming downe upon his Mill, then the Dam would hould, thought best in time, to fortifye the same, least all should be borne downe before he had taken his toule. Which haueing effected (makeing it the strongest place in the Country what with grate and small Gunns) he stands upon his gard, and refuseth to Surrender, but upon his owne terms; Which being granted, he secures the place till such time as S! William should, in parson, com and take possesion of the same: And was not this pritely, honestly, don, of a Miller.

The gratest difficulty, now to be performed, was to remove Drummond and Larance out of the way. These two Men was excepted out of the Governours pardon, by his Proclamation of Iune last, and severall papers since, and for to dye without Marcy. when ever taken: as they were the cheife Incendiarys, and promoters to, and for Bacons Designes; and by whose Councells all transactions were. for the grater part, managed all along on that Side. Drummond was formerly Gov-

Greene Spri[ng] secured for S[r] William.

Short carreer of Drummond & Larance.

ernour of Carolina, and all ways esteemed a Parson of such induments,
where Wisdom and honisty, are contending for supriority; which rendred him to be one of that sort of people, whose dementions are not to
be taken, by the line of an ordnary Capassety. Larance was late one
of the Assembley, and Burgis for Towne, in which he was a liver
He was a Parson not meanely aquainted with such learning (besides his
natureall parts) that inables a Man for the management of more then
ordnary imployments, Which he subjected to an eclips, as well in the
transactings of the present affaires, as in the darke imbraces of a
Blackamoore, his slaue: And that in so fond a Maner, as though Venus
was cheifely to be worshiped in the Image of a Negro: or that Buty
consisted all together in the Antiphety of Complections: to the noe
meane Scandle, and affrunt, of all the Vottrisses in or about towne.

When that West point was surrendred, and Greene Spring secur'd,

Drummond
& Coll.
Larance at
the Brick-
howse, in
New-Kent.

for the Governour, these two Gen! was at the Brick-howse, in New
Kent: a place Situate allmost oppossitt to West point, on the South
side of York River, and not 2 Miles removed from the said point, with
som Soulders under there Command; for to keepe the Governours Men
from landing on that Side; he haueing a Ship, at that time, at Ancor
nere the place. They had made som attempts to have hindred Granthams designes (of which they had gain'd som intilligence) but there
indeviours not fadging, they sent downe to Coll. Bacons to fetch of the
Gard there, under the Command of Whaley, to reinforce there owne
strength.*

Whaly was quickly won to obay the commands of his Masters,
especially such in whose servis he might expect to receue good Wages:
forth with drawing ou[t] his Men, amongst whom was Som Boys, all
laden with the goods, and last remanes of Coll. Bacons Estate, an[d]
with all posible Speed (after a March of 30 Miles,) joyne[d] with
Larance; where they Mustred in all (besides (Co[n]cubines and
Whores, Whaley haueing added his to the r[est?] about 300 Men
and Boys. With which number, being [too] weake for to desend downe
in to the heart of the Coun[trey,] (now clear'd of the Baconians, or
possest by the other [par]ty) they march up higher in to New Kent,
as far [as] Coll. Gouges, thinking (like the snow ball) to incr[ease by]
there rouleing. But finding that in stead of increas[ing] there number
decreast; and that the Moone of there fortune was now past the full,
they broke up how[se-]keeping, every one shifting for him selfe, as his

---

* The first edition of this narrative ends here.—Eds.

ta[ste?] or feares directed ; Whaly and Larance makein[g a] cleare escape ; but which way, or to what place, not knowne. Coll. Gouge and the rest, went to there own[e?] Howses. from whence they were brought upon there [tri]all, aborde a Ship, at Tindells point ; and from thence ([all] that were condem) [*sic*] sent to the place of Execution. [A]mongst which (of those that Suffer'd) were one M.ʳ H[all] Clarke of New Kent Court ; a parson of Neate Ingenuo[us] parts, but adicted to a more then ordnary prying in[to] the Secrits of State affaires, which som yeares las[t pa]st, wrought him in to the Governours [dis]pleasure. A[nd] which (tis posible) at this time was [not] forgott, [but] was lade to his charge upon his tria[ll(] which w[as by] a Court Martiall) to me is not visa[ble?] He nev[er hav]ing appear'd as a Soulder publickly, [yet] was co[ndemn'd] to be hang'd with 3 others (by Coll: [Bacons?]s howse, [viz.] Major Page, (once My Sarvant, at his [fir]st coming [into] the Countrey, Cap.ᵗ Yong, and one [Harris] . . . rtiall to Bacons Army.

This execution being over, the Govern[our] began to be wery of the Water : and findeing that he be[g]an to gether Strength, resalues to go a shore. There w[as] Considerable Cordialls administred to him, in litle more then a weekes [ti]me, which he found had don him a grate deale of [g]ood ; the Surrender of Wests point, Green spring, & [t]he death of the fore Mentioned Men. The place where [he] went on Shore, was at Coll: Bacons, now clem'd [or] the Rohella, by the hapey removeall of Whally, after [he] had (by the aideing helpe of his party) devovered [no] less then 2000 pounds (to my certaine knowledg) [of] Coll. Bacons estate ; the grater part in Store goods. [Here] he meets with M.ʳ Drummond, taken the day be[fore] in New Kent, where he had absconded, ever since [th]e brakeing up howse keepeing at Coll: Gouges. The [Govern]our . . . a more then ordnary gladness for to [see h]im, which (as he saide) did him more good then yᵉ [sigh]t of his owne Brother. If the Governour was soe [glad] to see Drummon, Drommon was no less sad to see [his h]onᵗ the sight of whom (with out the help of an As[trol]egr) might inform him what death he should [die,] and that he had not many days to live. That night [he] was sent aborde a Ship in Irons ; while the Governo.ʳ [re-]moved, the next day, in his Coach, to M.ʳ Brays : a [jour]nye of some 5 Miles. The next day after, being Sater[day.] Drummond was, by a party of Horss (who receu[ed him] at Coll: Bacons) convayed to his tryall : In his way [thi]ther he complained very much that his Irons hurt [him], and that his fine Cloake (as he called it, a green- . . . for

the H[a]ngman had taken his fur'd Coate from [him,] (a bad presage)
did much hinder him in his way. [When?] proffer'd [a h]orss, to
ride, he refused, and sade he [would] com to . . . e to his port before
he was preparde [wi]th his Anc[hor]: ading that he did very much
fere [S: Wil]liam w[ould] not al[low h]im time to put of his dir[ty
cl]othes b[efore] he went to lye downe upon his ev[en]ing b[e]d.
[He s]aide, welcom be the grace of God, for [it would clea]nse him
from all his filth and pollution. He ex[pressed] abundance of thankes
for being permitted to res[t hi]m selfe upon the Roade, while he
tooke a pipe of Tobacco. He discoursed very much, with that parson
who comm[anded] his gard, concerning the late troubles, affirming that
he was wholly innoscent of those . . .

[CÆTERA DESUNT.]